S0-DVG-572

Join my
Band!

— Doctor
Noize

Book Two of The Phineas McBoof Series
The Return Of Phineas McBoof

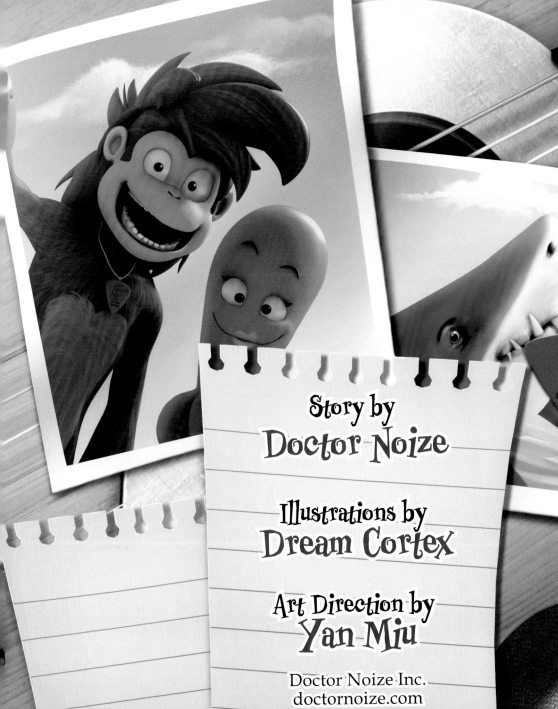

Story by
Doctor Noize

Illustrations by
Dream Cortex

Art Direction by
Yan Miu

Doctor Noize Inc.
doctornoize.com

Hear and sing this story with the album of the same name.

Read and hear the Band's first adventure in *The Ballad Of Phineas McBoof.*

But no matter what you do, do not go to **doctornoize.com** unless you wanna have fun and learn stuff.

THE WIZARDZ BEHIND THE CURTAIN...

Story & Creative Director	Doctor Noize
Art Director & Character Designer	Yan Miu
Original Character Designer	Christian Lowe
Concept Artist	Yan Miu
2D Production Artists	Cherry Leung, Gabriel Li, Icy Ngai, Chan Kai Chung, Hoi On Siu, Canny Sheh
3D Production Artists	Ken Cheng, Howard Lau, Carol Lee, Ming Him Chan, William Law, Cody Liu
Dream Cortex Project & Business Manager	Benjamin Yiu
Dream Cortex Creative Leader	Philip Lau
Doctor Noize Inc. Bizness & Sales (BS) Director	Brian McNulty
Photographer	Andrew Arkis
Text Editors	Adam Bock, Leola Cullinan
Executive Directors	Yat Siu, David Kim

INSPIRATION & THANKS

For the great adventurers Sidney Grace & Riley Max. It is my privilege to be a part of your journeys.

Thank you to the amazing team at Dream Cortex and BeTop for outdoing yourselves again. Yan — it's a joy to witness your genius produce new layouts. Special thanks to Cherry Leung, that rare combination of artistry, hard work, reliability, and boundless positive energy — a true delight. Much gratitude to Ken Cheng and Ben Yiu for demanding that we work until we get the Doctor Noize 3D model right — shades of me, but it also fits in with the other animated characters. You did it fellas! Thanks as usual to the Fab Five: Adam Bock, Craig Swanson, Weldon Dodd, Coert Voorhees, and Janette Cullinan. (Adam must be given kudos for "to hear some guy sing....")

No Doctor Noize production would exist without the unwavering commitment of Janette for years with no guarantees. Continued thanks to The International Band Of Misunderstood Geniuses for allowing me to be their imbedded journalist. I'm grateful to Brian McNulty, whose fine work, good humor, and "I'll take care of it" attitude allows me to focus on creative production. Special thanks to Yat Siu and Ray Chuk for taking a chance. And finally, to Dave Kim for not only his amazing belief and dedication, but for his deep and generous friendship too. Dave would appreciate it if you take him to a cheap family restaurant chain when he's in town, just like we did.

— Doctor Noize

LEGAL MUMBO JUMBO

Do not let any frogs, flamingos or ferrets claim they wrote this book. Isn't starring in the book enough? Do not ask Sidney The Beak to sing you happy birthday at your birthday party. It's not her thing. Ask Doctor Noize instead. You should still invite Sidney to the party, though — she'll make it more fun. If you like this book, please read it to all your friends, grandparents, cousins, goldfish, parents, computer games, plants, teachers, animated alter egos, dolls, recording devices, imaginary alien visitors, and BFF's. You'll be glad you did.

First Edition

ISBN: 978-0-9831259-1-4
Library of Congress Control Number: 2011935582
Doctor Noize Inc., Lone Tree, CO, 1-303-858-0007

Where, oh where, could Phineas be? Find out soon with his symphony.

There once was a monkey — McBoof was his name.
His fans called him Phineas, and he had great fame
On the Isle of Thelonious — but left it behind him
Before everyone but himself had defined him.

But that is the tale of another old book,
And you have come here for new stories and looks.
So suffice it to say McBoof started a Band
Of Misunderstood Geniuses from every land.

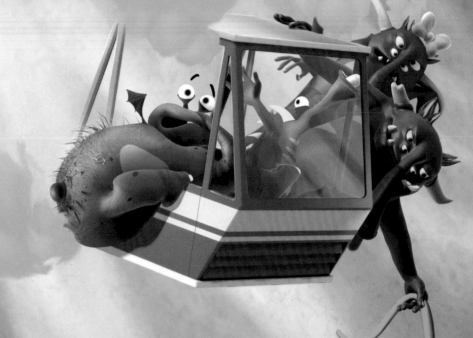

And just who were the members of this famous group?
While I'm sure that you know, just in case... here's the scoop:
'Twas a monkey, a robot, a hippo, a lizard,
Four monsters, and one eight-armed drummer girl wizard.

Let's catch up with their tour, let's find out where they're at.
Ask your mom, or your dad, or your dog, or your cat.
Are they *here*? Are they *there*? Where'd they go? Who knows *where*?
You should listen for music, and look for them there...

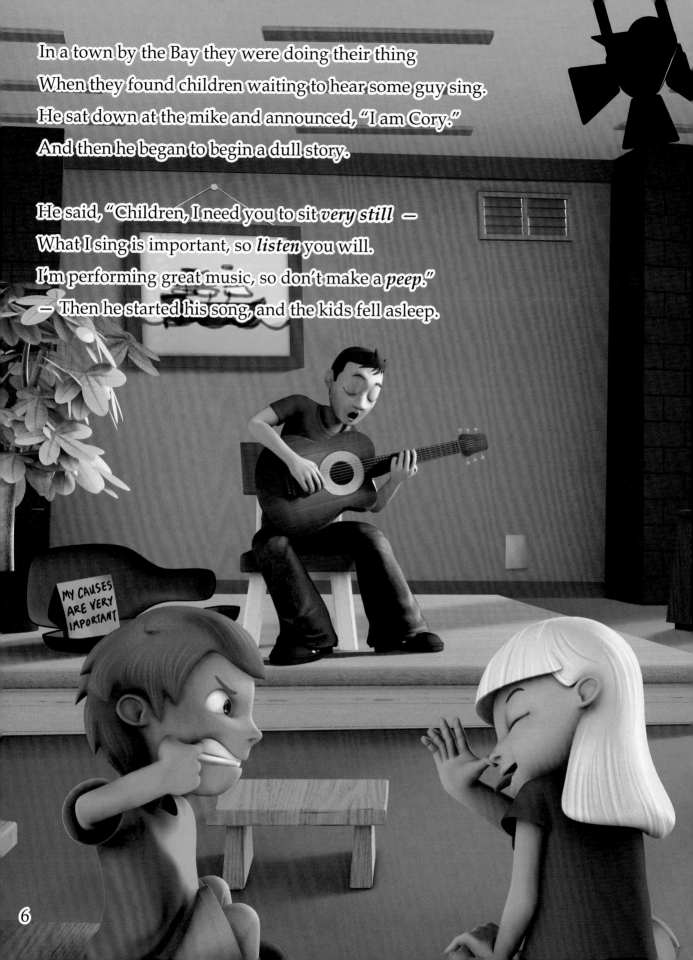

In a town by the Bay they were doing their thing
When they found children waiting to hear some guy sing.
He sat down at the mike and announced, "I am Cory."
And then he began to begin a dull story.

He said, "Children, I need you to sit *very still* —
What I sing is important, so *listen* you will.
I'm performing great music, so don't make a *peep*."
— Then he started his song, and the kids fell asleep.

MY CAUSES
ARE VERY
IMPORTANT

Well, our heroes had never seen something so boring.
And fearful the children would never stop snoring,
They grabbed all their instruments, raced to the stage,
And they sang, and they danced, and they grooved, and they played...

Then the *kids* — they woke up, and they jumped to their feet,

And they sang to the song, and they danced to the beat.

And the man watched in awe as kids screamed: **"One more song!"**

And he asked the Band after, "What did I do *wrong*?"

That's when Phineas said to him, "Man, you've got heart,
But the way you perform takes the fun out of art.
You've got something to sing, you've got something to say,
But the word that we use to make music is *play!*"

"It is good that you care, by all means have a point...
But first learn what to do to win over the joint.
Join my Band and experience musical joys —
We'll give you a fresh start and call you... *Doctor Noize!*"

9

In the Forest Of Foofaphones, high in the trees
Rang the glorious chirping of bird harmonies.
As the sounds of the songbirds soared into the sky,
They created a chorus of creatures who fly.

As they sang, every note was in twirps and in tweets.
It was wordless and wonderful, sugary sweet.
They were singing the way you've heard birds sing in song—
Until suddenly, one *other* voice came along...

She said,

Yo! Here I go! My name's Sidney The Beak!

From this bird is the word comin' straight with no squeak!

From the flapping of wings to the flow of the stream,

It is motion that guides me and words that I dream.

Now, the other birds paused in surprise at these words —
This was not really singing becoming of birds.
And the songbirds said, "Sidney The Beak, *stop* that yapping!"
But Sidney replied, "It's not yapping — it's *rapping!*"

"It's rhythm and rhyming that has my heart heard.
I don't hum, I don't sing — I just focus on words."
Now, our Band thought that Sidney was so hunky dunky
They wanted her in, so they turned to the monkey...

"Ape man," Sidney said, "If you're seeking a songbird,
I'll tell you straight up that you're picking the *wrong* bird."
"Oh, no, you're The One," McBoof said. "You're our flapper."
And that is how Sidney became the Band's rapper.

At the edge of the Forest, they came to a grotto
That echoed with singing in heavy vibrato
From three creatures having a bit of a fight
Over who got to stand in the cave's sole spotlight.

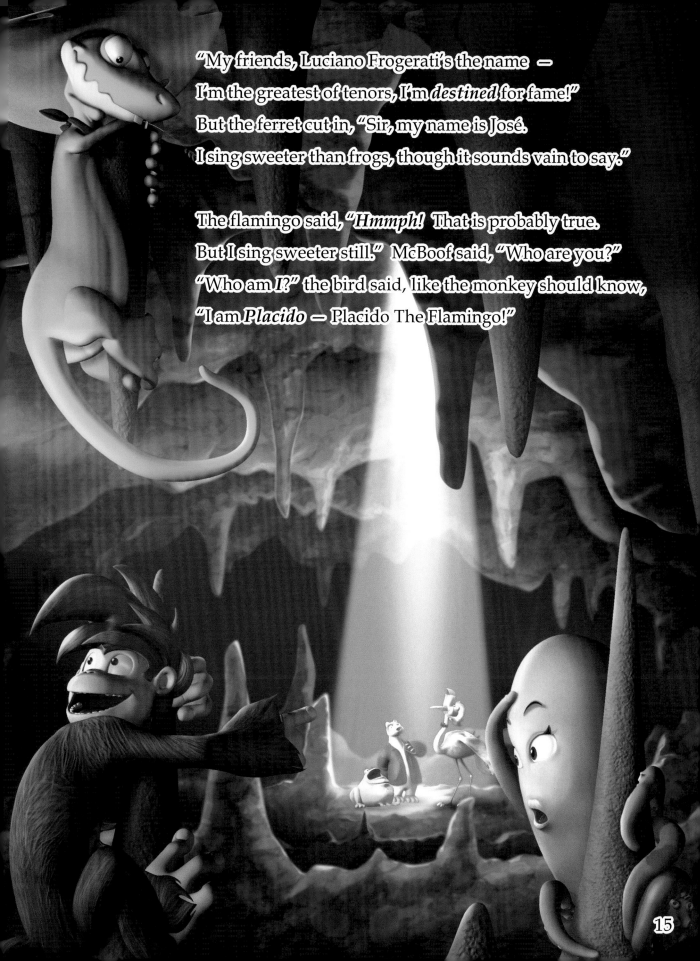

"My friends, Luciano Frogerati's the name —
I'm the greatest of tenors, I'm *destined* for fame!"
But the ferret cut in, "Sir, my name is José.
I sing sweeter than frogs, though it sounds vain to say."

The flamingo said, "*Hmmph!* That is probably true.
But I sing sweeter still." McBoof said, "Who are you?"
"Who am *I*?" the bird said, like the monkey should know,
"I am *Placido* — Placido The Flamingo!"

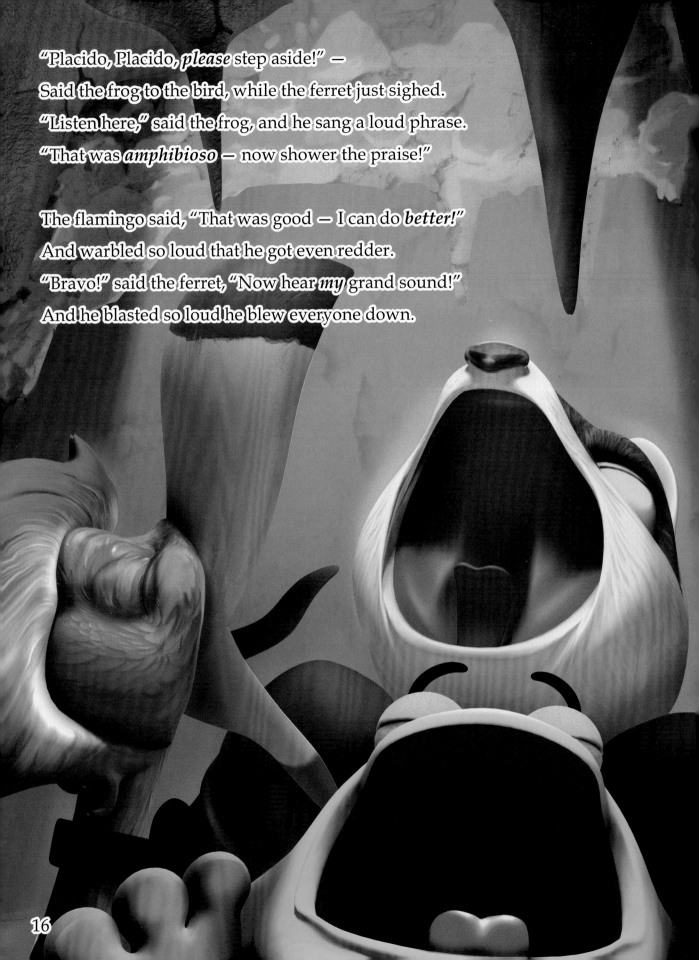

"Placido, Placido, *please* step aside!" —
Said the frog to the bird, while the ferret just sighed.
"Listen here," said the frog, and he sang a loud phrase.
"That was **amphibioso** — now shower the praise!"

The flamingo said, "That was good — I can do *better!*"
And warbled so loud that he got even redder.
"Bravo!" said the ferret, "Now hear *my* grand sound!"
And he blasted so loud he blew everyone down.

16

Then they started to argue, as each of the three
Shouted, *"I* am the best!" — *"I'm* the best!" — *"No, it's me!"*
And soon three different songs screamed in musical violence
'Til suddenly Phineas shouted out:

SILENCE!

"Now listen here, furball and froglegs and feathers:
You can all join my Band if you'll just sing togethers."
And suddenly silence was all that was heard —
The frog looked at the ferret, who looked at the bird.

They knew McBoof's Band was a fine place to sing,
So all three of them thought, and they thunk the same thing...
And they suddenly said simultaneously,
"Maestro Monkey... Will there be a solo for *me?*"

So McBoof and his great International Band
Of Misunderstood Geniuses went land to land.
And they gave people music, they played from their hearts —
They made people feel loved, and feel great, and feel smart.

All the while, they kept writing The World's Greatest Song.
They worked on it together, they worked hard and long.
It was very good work, it was very much fun.
Yes, they wrote and rewrote... 'Til one day it was *done*.

And then the Band voted — all thirteen to one —
A return to Thelonious would be great fun.
A return to the Isle of the great monkey's birth,
Just to give their Great Song its premiere on This Earth.

Now, word quickly spread that a concert was planned
Of the great P. McBoof and his mighty fine Band.
And all on the Island — from Aaron to Zak —
Were McThrilled that McBoof was McGoing to come back.

On the night of the concert, I'm sure you're aware,
Every monkey who lived on the Island was there.
And everyone's cousins and uncles and aunts
Started "*Phineas! Phineas! Phineas!*" chants.

When McBoof took the stage, the crowd screamed with delight,
And the sound of the screaming, it filled up the night.
So McBoof raised his hand and did silence the throng
And they all held their breath — 'til he started the song...

23

Yes, the monkey did sing, and the Band — it did play.
But no one heard The World's Greatest Song on that day.
'Cause the crowd of fine monkeys cheered so big and proud
That no musical group could make Noizes so loud.

When they finished The Song, the Band ran from the stage,
And they hopped on their boats and rowed quickly away.
But the crowd kept on cheering in giddy delight
— No one noticed they'd left 'til the end of the night.

And I just have to tell you, it just goes to show:
You may have a great plan, but you just never know.

Well...

McBoof was McBummed, there was no getting 'round it
They'd searched for The World's Greatest Song and they'd found it.
But nobody'd heard it, so nobody knew
What those notes, and those chords, and those lyrics could do.

So the Band cheered him up, and they sang him a song,
And McBoof cracked a smile, stood back up, sang along.
But come morning they found just a note in his place.
It was written as music, composed with great grace:

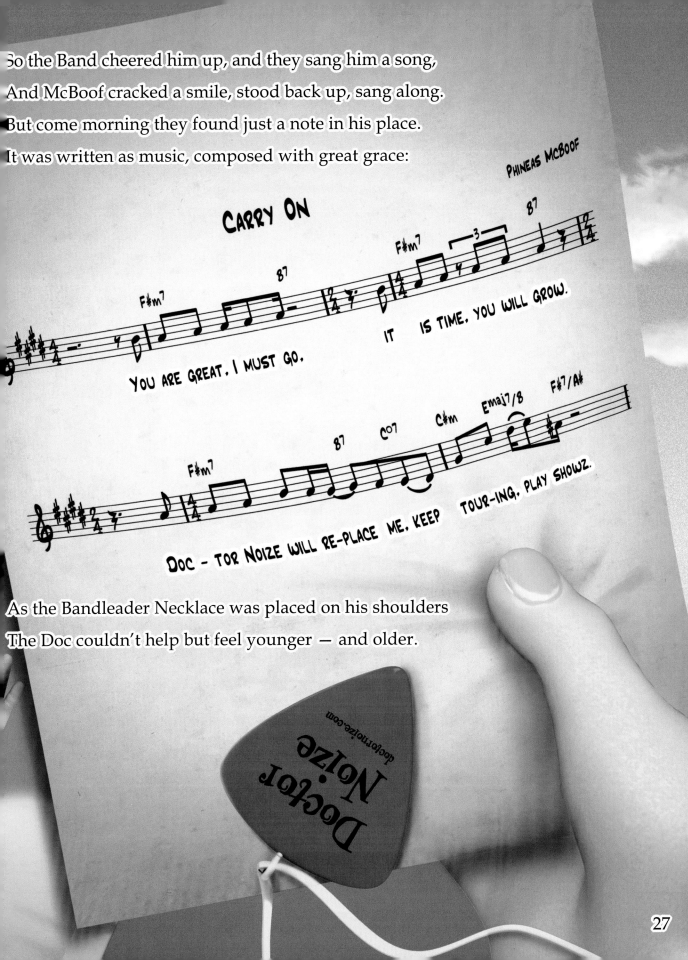

As the Bandleader Necklace was placed on his shoulders
The Doc couldn't help but feel younger — and older.

So...

Who knows where Doc Noize and his Band are right now?
Perhaps they're enjoying the mooing of cows,
Or the cooing of pigeons who sing in E minor,
Or ostriches oboeing — nothing is finer.

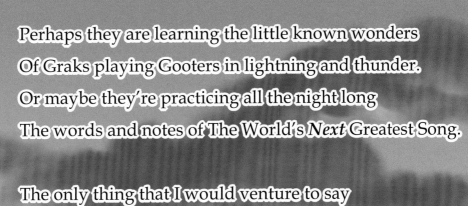

Perhaps they are learning the little known wonders
Of Graks playing Gooters in lightning and thunder.
Or maybe they're practicing all the night long
The words and notes of The World's *Next* Greatest Song.

The only thing that I would venture to say
Is that you should find something, and something to play.
You should go with your gut, you should play from your heart.
You should not worry much when folks say it ain't art.

Because then you'll be ready, and know what to do
If the moment arrives, and the Band passes through.
You'll see Sidney The Beak, Lenny Long Tail, Doc Noize
You'll see Riley The Robot with all her cool toyz.

Mister Boo, and Miss Ooh, and Miss Gah, and old Gus,
And a ferret, flamingo, and frog who will fuss.
You'll see Backbone and Bottomus backing the Band
And perhaps some who've joined since I last saw them jam.

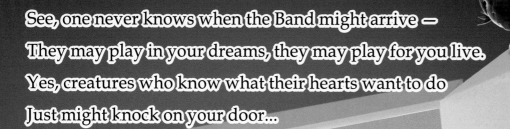

See, one never knows when the Band might arrive —
They may play in your dreams, they may play for you live.
Yes, creatures who know what their hearts want to do
Just might knock on your door...

...and ask *You* to join too.